STEM CAREERS
MECHANICAL ENGINEER

by Nikole Brooks Bethea

pogo

Ideas for Parents and Teachers

Pogo Books let children practice reading informational text while introducing them to nonfiction features such as headings, labels, sidebars, maps, and diagrams, as well as a table of contents, glossary, and index.

Carefully leveled text with a strong photo match offers early fluent readers the support they need to succeed.

Before Reading

- "Walk" through the book and point out the various nonfiction features. Ask the student what purpose each feature serves.
- Look at the glossary together. Read and discuss the words.

Read the Book

- Have the child read the book independently.
- Invite him or her to list questions that arise from reading.

After Reading

- Discuss the child's questions. Talk about how he or she might find answers to those questions.
- Prompt the child to think more. Ask: Do you know anyone who works as a mechanical engineer? What projects has he or she been involved in? Do you have any interest in this kind of work?

Pogo Books are published by Jump!
5357 Penn Avenue South
Minneapolis, MN 55419
www.jumplibrary.com

Library of Congress Cataloging-in-Publication Data

Names: Bethea, Nikole Brooks, author.
Title: Mechanical engineer / by Nikole B. Bethea.
Description: Minneapolis, MN: Jump!, Inc., [2017]
Series: STEM careers | Audience: Ages 7-10.
Includes bibliographical references and index.
Identifiers: LCCN 2017007350 (print)
LCCN 2017009933 (ebook)
ISBN 9781620317181 (hardcover: alk. paper)
ISBN 9781624965951 (ebook)
Subjects: LCSH: Mechanical engineering—Vocational guidance—Juvenile literature.
Mechanical engineers—Juvenile literature.
Classification: LCC TJ147 .B427 2017 (print)
LCC TJ147 (ebook) | DDC 621.023—dc23
LC record available at https://lccn.loc.gov/2017007350

Editor: Jenny Fretland VanVoorst
Book Designer: Molly Ballanger
Photo Researcher: Molly Ballanger, Kirsten Chang, & Leah Sanders

Photo Credits: Getty: Andersen Ross, 5; Erik Tham, 6-7; Hero Images, 8-9; Eric Raptosh Photography, 19. iStock: asiseeit, 18. Science Source: Science Source, 14-15; Philippe Psaila, 16-17. Shutterstock: Gergory Gerber, cover; Cineberg, 1; Dmytro Zinkevych, 3; SvedOliver, 10-11; lightwavemedia, 14-15; Nestor Rizhniak, 20-21; Baloncici, 23. SuperStock: Blend Images, 4.

Printed in the United States of America at Corporate Graphics in North Mankato, Minnesota.

TABLE OF CONTENTS

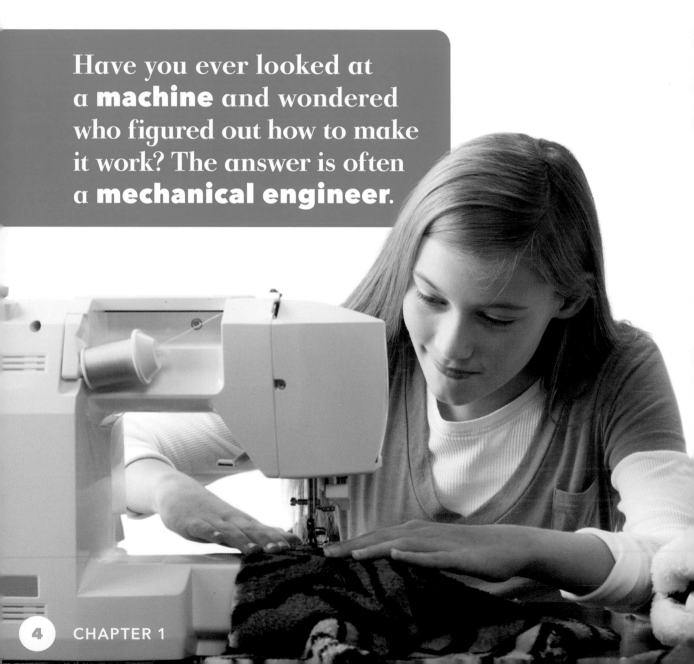

CHAPTER 1
MAKE IT WORK!

Have you ever looked at a **machine** and wondered who figured out how to make it work? The answer is often a **mechanical engineer**.

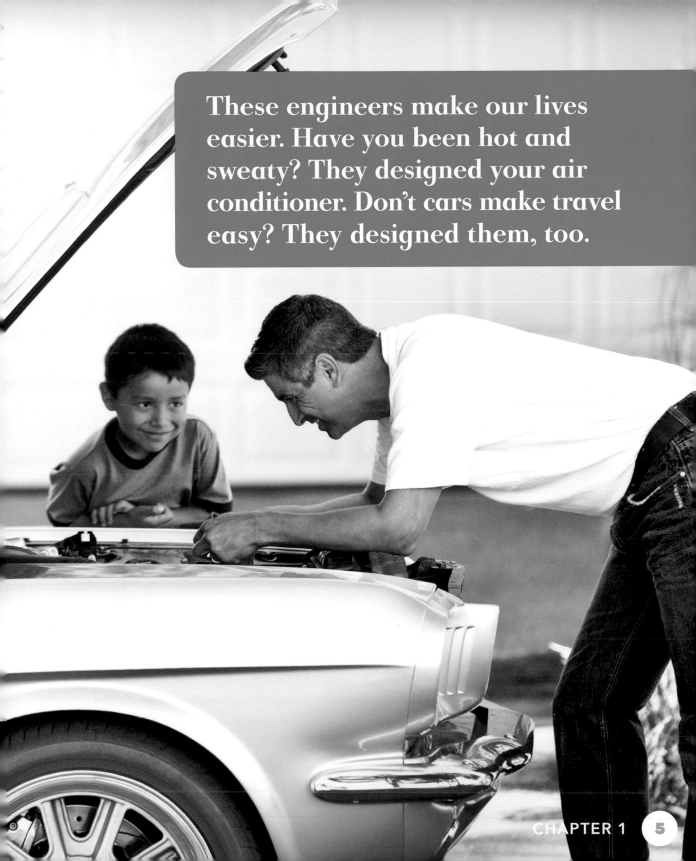

These engineers make our lives easier. Have you been hot and sweaty? They designed your air conditioner. Don't cars make travel easy? They designed them, too.

These engineers design and build mechanical **devices**. They use **physics** principles to solve problems. They are experts at using **forces**, **energy**, and motion to make things work.

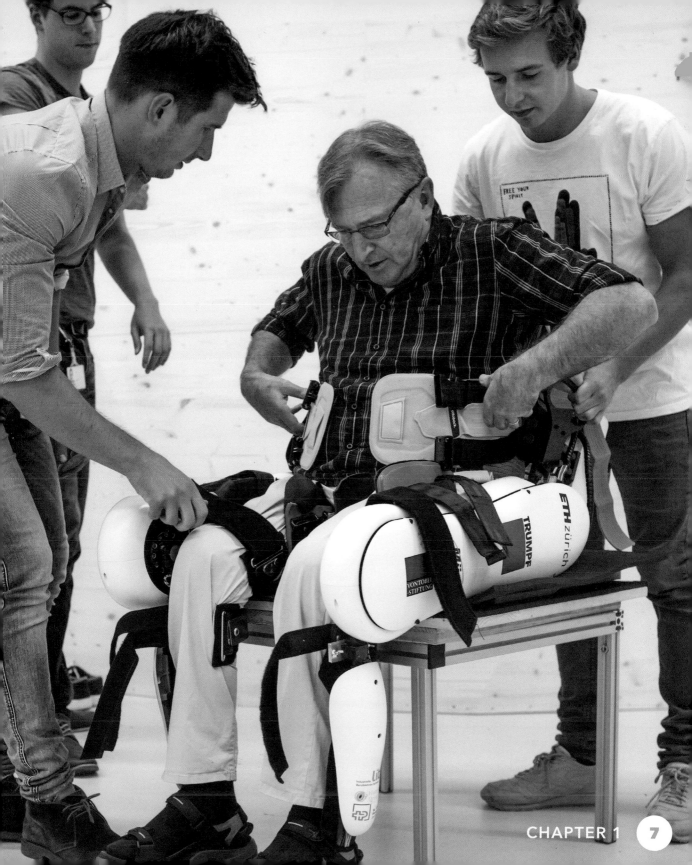

First they try to understand the problem that needs a solution. They think about how a machine might solve it. Then they design the device. They make a **prototype**. They test it. Finally they direct production.

DID YOU KNOW?

Prototype means "first model." It may not work at first. But engineers figure out what went wrong and why. They redesign. They try again.

CHAPTER 2

WHAT DO THEY DO?

Mechanical engineers work in many **industries**. Some work in power plants. They design and maintain **boilers**, **turbines**, and **generators**. They measure flows. They note temperatures. They record pressures. They improve how power is made.

power plant

TAKE A LOOK!

How is electric power made? Fuel is burned. It heats water. The water turns to steam. Pressure from the steam turns a turbine. It causes magnets to spin within wire coils. This creates electricity!

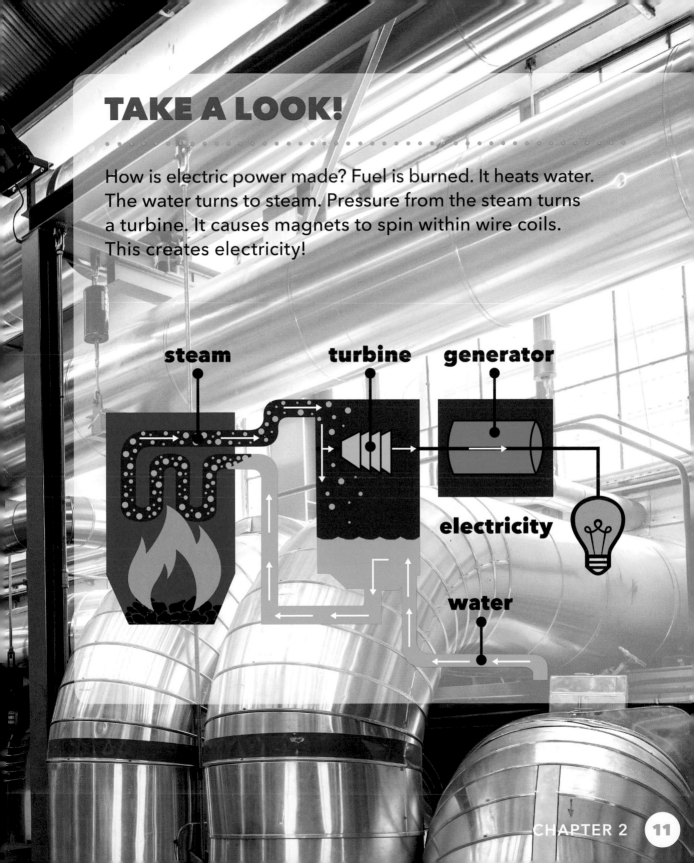

steam

turbine

generator

electricity

water

Some design building systems. They lay out the plumbing pipes. They design fire sprinkler systems. They determine the size of air conditioners and heaters needed. They estimate the cost to build the systems.

Some work for the space program. They help build robots. They develop new rocket fuels. They improve engine designs. They create computer models. They turn scientists' ideas into space missions.

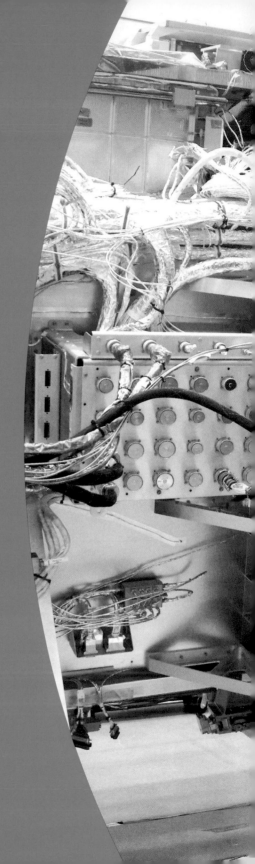

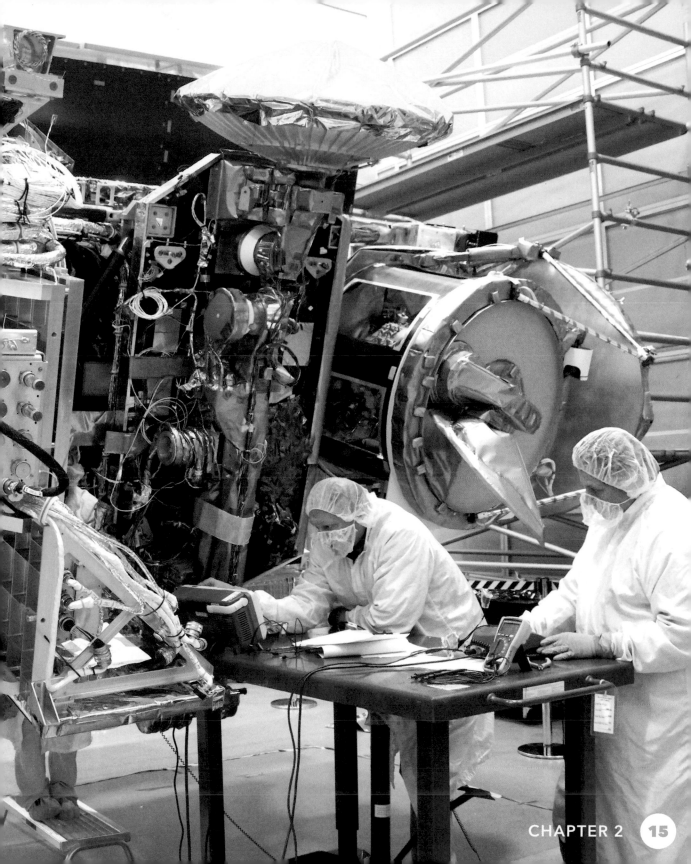

Mechanical engineers work as part of a team. **Architects** help with building plans. Doctors help them create new medical devices. **Electrical engineers** help power what they make.

CHAPTER 3

WHAT CAN YOU DO?

Do you like to solve problems? Do you like math and science? You could be an engineer. You will need a college degree. Then you must pass a test. This gives you a **license**.

What can you do now?
Focus on math and science.
Build a rocket kit.
Join a **robotics** club.

The future is bright. You might create artificial body parts. You might make robots that do the work of humans. You might find new energy sources. Mechanical engineers can change the world!

DID YOU KNOW?

To work in this field, you need STEM skills. What does STEM stand for? Science. Technology. Engineering. Math. STEM careers are in demand. They pay well, too.

ACTIVITIES & TOOLS

BALLOON ROCKET ACTIVITY

Now it's your turn to be a mechanical engineer. This activity allows you to design a rocket that you can launch.

What You Need:
- a balloon
- one wide straw (example: milkshake straw)
- one thin straw (must fit inside the wide straw)
- tape
- bull's-eye target drawn on paper or cardboard
- blunt-tip scissors

❶ **Build the launcher:** Slip 1–2 inches (3–5 centimeters) of the thin straw into the opening of the balloon. Tape the balloon tightly to the straw.

❷ **Build the rocket:** Using the wide straw, fold one tip over to seal it. Wrap tape around folded tip and straw.

❸ **Set your target:** Place bull's-eye target 5 feet (1.5 meters) away from you.

❹ **Launch:** Inflate balloon by blowing into the thin straw. Slide the wide straw (rocket) onto the thin straw (launcher). Ready. Aim. Fire!

❺ **Did you hit the target?** If not, try again by launching it at a different angle.

GLOSSARY

architects: People who design buildings and advise in their construction.

boilers: Fuel-burning containers that produce steam.

devices: Pieces of equipment that serve a special purpose.

electrical engineers: People who use electricity to create solutions to society's problems and make things that humans use.

energy: The ability to do work.

forces: Pushes or pulls.

generators: Machines that produce electricity.

industries: Businesses or manufacturers that provide a particular product or service.

license: Permission to do something granted by a qualified authority.

machine: A combination of parts that transmit forces, motion, and energy to do some desired work.

mechanical engineer: An engineer who applies principles of force, motion, and energy and knowledge of manufacturing and operational processes to advance the world.

physics: The science that deals with matter and energy and their actions upon each other.

prototype: An original model on which something is patterned.

robotics: The technology involved in the design, construction, and operation of robots.

turbines: Devices that convert the energy of a moving fluid into rotary motion to spin a generator.

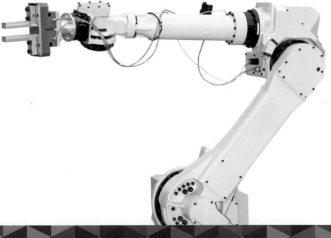

INDEX

TO LEARN MORE

Learning more is as easy as 1, 2, 3.

1) Go to www.factsurfer.com

2) Enter "mechanicalengineer" into the search box.

3) Click the "Surf" button to see a list of websites.

With factsurfer, finding more information is just a click away.